Writing with the Five-Paragraph Model

Grades 6–8

Frank Schaffer Publications®

Author: Delana Heidrich
Editors: Linda Triemstra, Raymond Wiersma

Frank Schaffer Publications®

Printed in the United States of America. All rights reserved. Limited Reproduction Permission: Permission to duplicate these materials is limited to the person for whom they are purchased. Reproduction for an entire school or school district is unlawful and strictly prohibited. Frank Schaffer Publications is an imprint of School Specialty Publishing. Copyright © 2004 School Specialty Publishing.

Send all inquiries to:
Frank Schaffer Publications
8720 Orion Place
Columbus, OH 43240-2111

Writing with the Five-Paragraph Model—grades 6–8

ISBN: 0-7696-3402-8

2 3 4 5 6 7 8 9 10 POH 10 09 08 07 06

Table of Contents

Introduction	4–5
What Is a Paragraph?	6–7
What Is the Five-Paragraph Writing Model?	8–9
The Five-Paragraph Writing Process	10–11
Evaluating the Assignment	12–13
Conducting Research	14–15
Tracking Research	16–17
Referencing Your Sources	18–19
Brainstorming and Organizing	20–21
Writing the Introduction: Developing a Thesis Statement	22–23
Writing the Introduction: Using an Anecdote	24–25
Writing the Introduction: Using Quotations	26–27
Writing the Introduction: Starting with a Question	28–29
Writing the Body: Developing Topic Sentences	30–31
Writing the Body: Using Details	32–33
Writing the Body: Using Examples	34–35
Writing the Body: Using Sequencing	36–37
Writing the Body: Using Importance and Necessity	38–39
Writing the Conclusion	40–41
Writing the Conclusion: Combining Styles	42–43
Analyzing the Five-Paragraph Model	44–45
Descriptive Writing: Record and Write	46–47
Evaluating Fiction: Analyzing Aesop	48–49
Evaluating Nonfiction: Behind Every Great Man	50–51
Writing a Report	52–53
Descriptive Writing	54–55
Evaluating Fiction	56–57
Evaluating Nonfiction	58–59
Writing a Report	60–61
How Did I Do?	62
Go Team!	63
Answer Key	64

INTRODUCTION

The five-paragraph writing model can serve your students well. Five-paragraph writings can satisfy the requirements of middle school assignments across the curriculum. Students can analyze characters and summarize literary works using the five-paragraph model. They can report on famous events and personalities in five-paragraph format. They can compare, contrast, clarify, instruct, justify, predict, prove, evaluate, and draw conclusions all using the five-paragraph model—that is, of course, if they can compose an effective five-paragraph writing.

Writing with the Five-Paragraph Model can help your middle school students master the five-paragraph model. In two-page lessons, it introduces students to the five-paragraph format and walks them through the steps of using it effectively.

Students learn to research, reference, brainstorm, and organize a five-paragraph writing. They learn to write introductory, body, and concluding paragraphs in a variety of styles. Then they compose five-paragraph writings with assistance, and finally they write five-paragraph papers on their own.

Use *Writing with the Five-Paragraph Model* in the instruction of a complete unit on writing five-paragraph essays, or assign individual lessons to reinforce specific skills in your students. Either way, your students will benefit from reading, writing, discussing, and interacting with the thorough explanations and engaging activities found within these pages.

The five-paragraph model helps students to learn writing skills or to sharpen writing skills they already have. To encourage your students to write, you may want them to keep a portfolio of their best work. Portfolios help students to judge the quality of their work and give them the opportunity to share their work with readers other than their teachers or peers.

When students choose writing samples for their portfolios, they will want to select the pieces they consider to be their best. In addition to pieces written specifically in the five-paragraph format, these types of writing are among those that might be included in a portfolio:

poetry	short stories	letters
research papers	journal entries	reports
book reports	movie reviews	reading logs

Name _____ Date _____

 # THE FIVE-PARAGRAPH WRITING PROCESS

Directions: Answer the following questions about the five-paragraph writing process.

1. What are some steps you can take to be sure you understand the assignment before you begin?

   _____

   _____

2. List five sources you might use to research the life accomplishments of Benjamin Franklin.

   _____

   _____

3. What source would you examine to answer the following questions: Did you like the story *Charlotte's Web*? Why or why not?

   _____

   _____

4. What methods have you used to brainstorm ideas for writing in the past?

   _____

   _____

5. Why is it important to organize your ideas before beginning a five-paragraph writing?

   _____

   _____

 ## PERSONAL PRACTICE

Think of an athlete, writer, or artist you like. What kind of five-paragraph essay could you write about this person? What research sources could you use in writing your essay? How would you brainstorm? How might you organize your research and ideas?

Published by Frank Schaffer Publication. Copyright protected. 0-7696-3402-8 *Writing with the Five-Paragraph Model*

Evaluating the Assignment

Five-paragraph writings can satisfy the requirements of many assignments. But before you start writing, be sure you know what is being asked of you. Clue words within writing prompts and essay questions hint at what your answer should look like.

Explain/Define
Your response to a prompt that asks you to explain or define should be merely explanatory. Divide your explanation or definition into three components in the introductory paragraph. Address one component in each paragraph in the body of your work. Conclude by restating your introduction in a new way.

Summarize/Identify
The words *summarize* and *identify* ask you to derive your response from a given source. Refer to the source often in the body of your paper. A chronological approach works well when you are asked to summarize.

Predict/Draw Conclusions
These words ask you to evaluate a given source and move beyond it. In the introduction, summarize your source and state your prediction or conclusion. In the body, solidly support three reasons for your prediction or conclusion. In the conclusion, defend your points in a strong statement that refers to the "proves" given in the body.

Compare/Contrast/Describe
These words ask for a descriptive rather than explanatory or persuasive response. Use figurative language, imagery, and highly descriptive adverbs and adjectives in a response to a request to compare, contrast, or describe. Remember that comparisons are similarities and contrasts are differences.

Evaluate/Review/Analyze
When you are asked to evaluate, review, or analyze, you are asked to examine, make judgments, and support opinions. Break your judgments or opinions into three clear categories in the introduction. Use lots of examples, references, and/or expert opinions to support your judgments in the body. Strongly state your overall opinion in the persuasive way in the conclusion.

Prove/Justify
These words ask for a persuasive response. State your main point clearly in the introduction. Support three subpoints with solid facts, examples, and reliable references in the body. Conclude with a persuasive statement.

Name _____ Date _____

 Evaluating the Assignment

Directions: The following excerpts are from five-paragraph writings. Match each excerpt with the question it attempts to answer. Then decide whether each excerpt is from the *introduction*, *body*, or *conclusion* of a five-paragraph writing. Indicate your responses on the lines provided.

Define the word *freedom*.	Describe your bedroom.
Write a review of your favorite movie.	Prove the existence of gravity.

_____ 1. The textures in my bedroom include rough, smooth, and everything in between. Soft, cuddly teddy bears rest on my fluffy down pillow. Oily, crunchy potato chip crumbs greet the feet of intruders who dare walk barefoot on my tickly, tall, shag carpet. A smooth wall-papered east wall smiles smugly at the three surrounding prickly stucco-textured walls. Even a close-eyed walk through my room is an adventure.

_____ 2. Throw a ball up, and it comes back down. Trip over a log, and you fall to the ground. Why? Because of a phenomenon called gravity. Sir Isaac Newton knew there was a reason apples fall off trees. His explorations suggested the existence of gravity. Experiments to follow confirmed his theory. Scientists today can even predict the behavior of gravity using precise measurements and formulas.

_____ 3. Its special effects are dramatic and convincing. Its dialogue is engaging and clever. Its characters are complex and developed. You can see why *Tornado Town, USA* is my all-time favorite movie.

_____ 4. Second, freedom means equal opportunities for all races and religions. Without the civil freedoms to vote, acquire gainful employment, and frequent any and all public places, freedom from captivity means nothing. Our nation could not boast the freedom of its minorities until the passage of the Civil Rights Act in the 1960s.

CONDUCTING RESEARCH

Some five-paragraph writings will require little or no research. Some will require a thorough examination of a single source. Others will require extensive research.

After you have evaluated your assignment, decide how much research it requires. If the assignment asks for your opinion about a general knowledge topic, you probably will not need to complete much research. If the assignment asks you to discuss a specific source, such as a story you read for homework or a movie you watched in class, then you need to understand the source on many levels. Take written or mental notes on facts, assumptions, style, purpose, and other details about the given source. If you are asked to report on a topic that takes you beyond your opinion or a single, specific source, you will need to complete extensive research. Consider many sources when completing research.

Reference Books
Reference books, including atlases, encyclopedias, guides, and dictionaries, offer general information about broad topics. Reading them can help you get an overall picture of your topic.

Nonfiction Books, Magazines, and Newspapers
For more detailed information on your topic, refer to nonfiction books, magazines, and newspapers. Look up your topic in the card catalog in your school library. Also locate your topic in subject-related indexes and tables of contents. For example, if you are researching the topic of light waves, you might look up the phrase *light waves* in the index of books about general science, physical science, or light.

Internet Sites
Internet sites can be especially useful in locating information on current events and personalities. Be aware, however, that the Internet has very few checks and balances. Anyone can publish anything on the Internet, so not all sources are reliable. When possible, choose sites that are sponsored by reliable sources such as universities, official organizations, and well-known institutions. When information is found on a questionable site, verify it with several other sites and present it as probable instead of factual when you write your report.

Nonprinted Materials
Nonfiction television and radio programs, personal interviews, and documentary movies are among the many nonprint reference materials that you might consider when researching a given topic. Think beyond books when you are in the research stage of your five-paragraph writing process.

Name _____ Date _____

CONDUCTING RESEARCH

Directions: Complete these practice research activities in your school's library and/or computer lab.

1. Write here three web addresses of reliable sources of information on heart disease.

Address 1: _____

Address 2: _____

Address 3: _____

2. Find the term *amino acids* in the index of three books. Record the book titles and page numbers where the term appears.

Book 1, pages: _____

Book 2, pages: _____

Book 3, pages: _____

3. Record here the titles of three chapters from books on health or nutrition that address the benefits of aerobic exercise.

Chapter title: _____

Chapter title: _____

Chapter title: _____

4. In a guide to cable television programs, locate one program title that suggests it will present factual information about an animal.

Title of the program: _____

Animal addressed: _____

5. Whom might you interview to gain information on living conditions during the Great Depression?

_____

_____

_____

Published by Frank Schaffer Publication. Copyright protected.   15   0-7696-3402-8 *Writing with the Five-Paragraph Model*

TRACKING RESEARCH

Organization is the key if you are conducting extensive research. The process can be divided into steps:

1. Locate appropriate sources.

2. Skim each source for useful information.

3. Read thoroughly the useful sections of the source.

4. Take notes on large notecards.

Effective notecard notes contain the following information.

1. **Subtopic:** Title each notecard with a word or phrase that captures the single subtopic of information you will record on the card. You may end up with many cards with the same subtopic. You may also use several cards with separate subtopics to cover all of the information in a single source.

2. **Information:** Jot information from a single source on a single subtopic on each card. Use quotation marks when recording a direct quote. Do not worry about punctuation or sentence structure; phrases are fine. These are just your reminder notes. You can return to the source if you need specifics later.

3. **Source:** Reference the source where you found your information using the referencing style your teacher wants to see in your paper's bibliography.

Sample Notecard for a Paper Summarizing the Life of O. Henry

> Subtopic: Childhood Challenges
>
> Information:
> Birthname: William Sidney Porter
> Birthdate: 1862
>
> Father was an alcoholic. Mother was in poor health. Mother died when William was three. Reared by grandparents and an aunt. Left school at age ten and went to work in a local pharmacy.
>
> Source:
> Mockridge, Carson. *The Life and Death of O. Henry*. New York: Farmhouse Publishing, 2003. 32–34.

Name _____   Date _____

 # TRACKING RESEARCH

Directions: Practice completing notecard research by completing the cards below. You will need to find a source in your school's library to help you complete the cards.

Essay Prompt: Evaluate the work ethic of Thomas Edison.

Subtopic: The Invention of the Lightbulb

Information:

Source:

Subtopic: Work Procedures at the Factory in Menlo Park

Information:

Source:

Referencing Your Sources

When you begin writing your five-paragraph work, you will refer to some of the research you have completed. Be sure to let your reader know when you are offering an idea that is not your own.

Citing Information Within Your Paper
Each time you refer to an idea that is not your own in your five-paragraph paper, cite your source, even if you have not used a direct quote. State the author's name and the page numbers on which you found the information.

Samples
Slee Kabbala (198–199) suggests there is no objective reality.

In a 2004 study of bipolar patients (Seaton, 243–257) . . .

Referencing Sources at the End of Your Work
At the end of your paper, reference your sources in a bibliography. You may wish to follow these guidelines.

1. Bibliographies are arranged alphabetically by author's last name.

2. For book entries, list information in the following order: author, title, place of publication, name of publishing house, date of publication.

3. For magazine and newspaper articles, list information in this order: author, title of article, title of magazine or newspaper, date of issue, page numbers of story.

4. For Internet sites, list information in this order: author, article title, web address, date accessed.

5. For nonprinted material, include all pertinent information.

Book Sample
Gardner, Howard. *The Shattered Mind.* New York: Vintage Books, 1976.

Magazine Article Sample
Heffelfinger, Derrick. "How to Raise Healthy Guinea Pigs." *House Pets Magazine.* May 14, 2004, 143–147.

Internet Site Sample
Jacobs, Dr. Michael. "Heart Health Now." www.healthyheart.com, accessed March 5, 2003.

Interview Sample
Zebber, Jonathan. Telephone interview, June 22, 2003.

Name _____   Date _____

 # REFERENCING YOUR SOURCES

Directions: You have used the following sources in a five-paragraph paper about the history of psychology. Create a bibliography listing your sources correctly.

Behaviorism written by John B. Watson and published by W. W. Norton and Company in New York, copyright 1958.

The Mind's New Science written by Howard Gardner in 1985 and published in New York by Basic Books Inc.

The J. N. Isbister book titled *Freud: An Introduction to His Life and Work* published in 1985 by Polity Press in New York.

Helen Swick Perry's work *Psychiatrist of America: The Life of Harry Stack Sullivan* published by the Belknap Press of Cambridge, Massachusetts, in 1982.

The Essential Jung selected and introduced by Anthony Storr and published by Princeton University Press in Princeton, New Jersey, in 1983.

Bibliography

BRAINSTORMING AND ORGANIZING

Once you have written down everyone else's ideas on notecards, it is time to let your creativity shine. How you choose to organize information is up to you. Use your own methods of brainstorming to help you decide how your research can best address your assignment requirements. Your goals in organizing your notes and information are to

1. select a main idea for your paper that addresses your assignment prompt or question. Write a thesis statement that expresses that idea.

2. select three subtopics that can be developed from your thesis.

3. decide how you will support each subtopic.

4. determine how you will conclude your paper.

How you reach those goals is up to you. Some options follow.

Notecard Shuffle
Create piles with notecards that contain similar subtopics. What main topic and subtopics emerge? Which three subtopics can your information support most convincingly?

Off to a Good Start
Some people get a clear picture of their overall paper by developing a great start. If you would like to try this approach, begin by writing your introductory paragraph. Be sure it includes a thesis statement and a hint at three subtopics that the body of your paper will support. Now look through your cards to see what information you have to support your claims.

Getting a Clear Picture
Some learning types work best when they can see an assignment visually. Create graphs, charts, idea webs, and book maps if these help you organize your thoughts. As you create a picture of your paper, look for a thesis, subtopics, supporting ideas, and conclusions to emerge.

Outline to Success
You might find it helpful to create a structured outline of your paper before you begin to write. Create one heading for each of the five paragraphs you will write. Then determine what supports will fit under each heading. Your outline will likely use words and phrases rather than complete sentences.

Name _____   Date _____

 # BRAINSTORMING AND ORGANIZING

Directions: Select a character from any story in your literature book for this activity. Imagine you have been asked to write a five-paragraph description of the character. Complete the webs below that could help you organize information about the character.

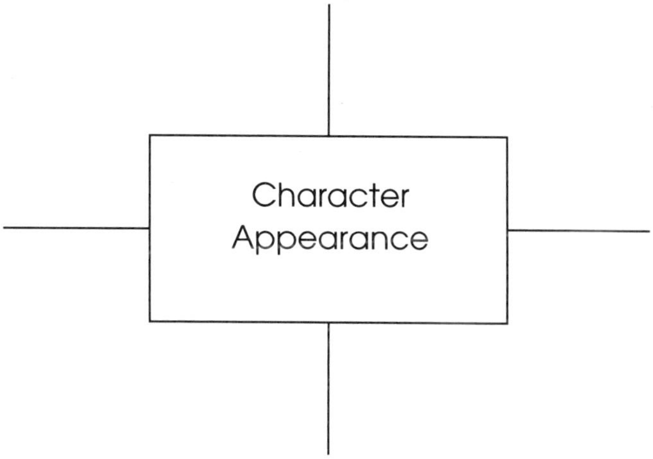

Character Appearance

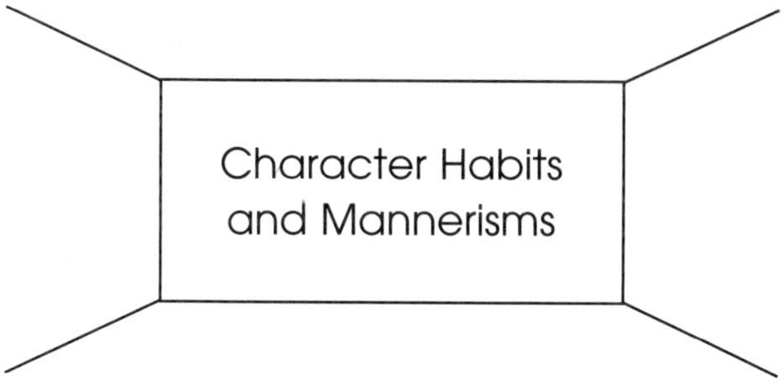

Character Habits and Mannerisms

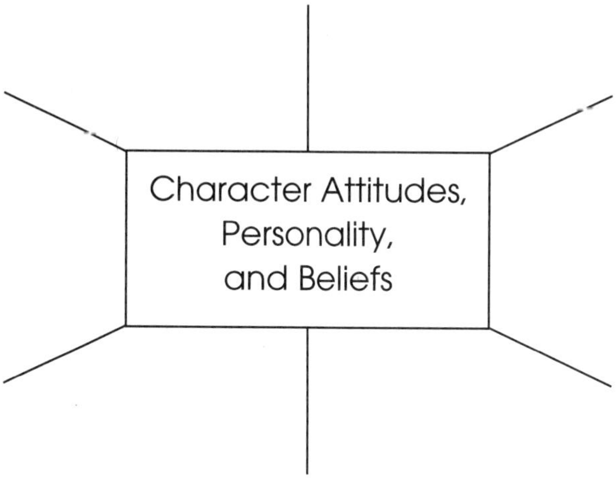

Character Attitudes, Personality, and Beliefs

Writing the Introduction: Developing a Thesis Statement

A **thesis statement** introduces your paper's topic and divides it into three subtopics that will be addressed in the body of the paper. A thesis statement can be made up of one or several sentences. Occasionally, a thesis statement is the entire introductory paragraph. More often, it is only a part of it. A thesis statement that does not make up the entire introduction can appear at the beginning, middle, or end of the paragraph.

In the following samples, the thesis statement is underlined.

Prompt 1: Write about your favorite sport.

Sample 1
Baseball is my favorite sport. I enjoy pitching on the school team. I love attending major league games. I am obsessed with baseball statistics and trivia.

Prompt 2: How does an air conditioner work?

Sample 2
It's 102 degrees outside. You're sitting in your living room, out of the sun but unable to get away from the heat. You are dripping with sweat and unable to muster the energy to do a thing. Then you remember the new air conditioner your dad installed. You flip it on and smile. How is your air conditioner able to cool you? It involves vents, a compressor, and a fan.

Prompt 3: Analyze the story of *James and the Giant Peach*.

Sample 3
Roald Dahl wrote outlandish tales for children of all ages. One of his most fanciful fantasies is *James and the Giant Peach*. To understand the story, a reader needs to evaluate the setting, the characters, and the plot.

Name _____ Date _____

WRITING THE INTRODUCTION: DEVELOPING A THESIS STATEMENT

Directions: Write an introductory paragraph in response to each of the prompts presented here. Underline the sentence or sentences that are your thesis statement.

1. Write a five-paragraph essay about your favorite author.

_____
_____
_____
_____

2. Write a persuasive essay arguing that web pages and e-mail will replace books and snail mail.

_____
_____
_____
_____

3. Describe your bedroom.

_____
_____
_____
_____

PERSONAL PRACTICE

Ask a friend to give you a writing prompt. Write an introductory paragraph, and underline the thesis statement. Then have your friend to do the same. How do your paragraphs differ? How are they the same?

WRITING THE INTRODUCTION: USING AN ANECDOTE

The introduction of a five-paragraph writing must state a thesis and alert readers to the three subtopics that will be addressed in the body. It should also grab readers' attention and pull them into the paper. One way to do that is to begin with an anecdote or brief story. This approach is equally effective in persuasive, descriptive, and informative works. Usually the anecdote begins the paragraph and is followed by the thesis statement and the description of the three subtopics.

Persuasive Sample
The year was 1964. My uncle was eating a piece of cake at his fortieth birthday party when he dropped his fork and clutched his chest. The next week at his funeral, my grandmother remarked that Uncle Kevin's young demise could not be prevented. "There's nothing you can do to stop a heart attack," she said. Today, we know better. Healthy eating habits, regular exercise, and stress reduction can all help you cut down your risk of a heart attack.

Descriptive Sample
Yesterday started out like any other winter weekday. I slapped my screaming alarm clock, hit the floor with both feet, and jumped into the shower. As usual, I was running late for school. Unlike usual, it didn't matter. According to the radio announcer I listened to as I gathered my school books, school had been cancelled on account of a snowstorm. So I put my backpack away and got out my snow boots and coat. What I experienced during the next four hours was glorious. The sights, sounds, and smells of winter enveloped me during a long, leisurely walk into the snowy woods behind my house.

Informative Sample
My first venture into deep water was not a pleasant one. My father tossed me into the deep end of a swimming pool in the general direction of my mother. My mother, arms stretched out and legs kicking, missed me altogether. Two minutes, much panic, and one scream for the lifeguard later, I found myself lying on the deck of the pool, my parents discussing swimming lessons above my head. Water safety requires awareness, training, and common sense.

Name _____   Date _____

 # Writing the Introduction: Using an Anecdote

Directions: Try your hand at writing introductions using anecdotes from your life as a starting point.

1. Write an introduction to a paper describing the adventures of camping.

_____
_____
_____
_____

2. Write an introduction to a paper convincing readers to get their homework turned in before deadlines.

_____
_____
_____
_____

3. Write an introduction to a paper teaching the rules of a sport.

_____
_____
_____
_____

 ## Personal Practice

Ask a friend to tell an anecdote from his or her life. Then tell your friend an anecdote from your life. What kinds of papers could you write using these anecdotes?

Writing the Introduction: Using Quotations

Using quotations in an introduction can set the mood, introduce the topic, or spark curiosity. Quotations are especially effective in the introduction of biographical works and inspirational papers. Quotations can appear at the beginning, middle, or end of an introductory paragraph.

Quote at the Beginning Sample
When Confucius said, "It does not matter how slowly you go so long as you do not stop," he must have had me in mind. I was almost two years old before I learned to walk. It took me five years of swimming lessons to be any good at the sport. And after twelve years of gymnastics, I still strive to improve. Perfecting physical skills takes patience, instruction, and—most importantly—a refusal to give up!

Quote in the Middle Sample
An illness in infancy left Helen Keller unable to see or hear. At first, Helen complained. In her dark and quiet world, she became frustrated easily. Then she changed her attitude and changed her life. "Although the world is full of suffering," she once said, "it is full also of the overcoming of it." Helen's life was full of overcoming. As a child, she learned to read Braille and speak English. As a young adult, she accomplished academic goals, including graduation from college. As an older adult, she inspired others to reach for their dreams, too.

Quote at the End Sample
For a democracy to be effective, its qualified voters must vote. Its citizens must communicate with their elected officials. And its elected officials must listen. After all, "democracy is a device that ensures we shall be governed no better than we deserve" (George Bernard Shaw).

Name _____ Date _____

Writing the Introduction: Using Quotations

Directions: Develop the following quotations and thesis statements into complete introductory paragraphs.

1. *Thesis Statement:* My favorite vacation spots in the United States include the middle of Montana, high in the Rocky Mountains, and far out into the sand of Death Valley.
   Quotation: "In the United States there is more space where nobody is than where anybody is. That is what makes America what it is" (Gertrude Stein).

   _____
   _____
   _____
   _____

2. *Thesis Statement:* A new book provides comfort, entertainment, and adventure.
   Quotation: "Wear the old coat and buy the new book" (Austin Phelps).

   _____
   _____
   _____
   _____

3. *Thesis Statement:* Making friends requires time, attention, and selflessness.
   Quotation: "You can make more friends in two months by becoming interested in other people than you can in two years by trying to get other people interested in you" (Dale Carnegie).

   _____
   _____
   _____
   _____

Writing the Introduction: Starting with a Question

Starting an introduction with a question provokes thought, piques curiosity, and directs attention to the thesis topic. Starting with a question is equally effective in writings intending to persuade, describe, or inform.

Sample Prompt: Write a review of the book *Scrooge, the Early Years*.

Sample Introductory Paragraph Starting with a Question
Have you ever wondered why Ebenezer Scrooge was such a grump in *A Christmas Carol*? *Scrooge, the Early Years* answers this question and more. In beautifully flowing prose, the author contextualizes Dickens's classic by revisiting events the Ghost of Christmas Past never thought to show you. Divided into chapters titled "Childhood," "The Working Years," and "Old Anger," *Scrooge, the Early Years* is thought-provoking and fun.

Sample Prompt: Tell the story behind the invention of the teabag.

Sample Introductory Paragraph Starting with a Question
Why are coffee grounds sold in round tin cans and tea grounds in little square teabags? The story of the tea bag is one of chance and error. It begins with a money-saving idea, moves on to an unexpected brewing technique, and ends with big-time success.

Sample Prompt: Describe your best friend.

Sample Introductory Paragraph Starting with a Question
What does it take to be a best friend? My best friend Fredrick knows the answer. He is thoughtful and considerate. He is always there for me. He is open and honest.

Name _____ Date _____

 **WRITING THE INTRODUCTION: STARTING WITH A QUESTION**

Directions: Write an introductory paragraph that begins with a question to begin a paper for each of the following prompts.

1. Describe your favorite relative.

_____
_____
_____

2. Convince me that either males or females have it easier in life.

_____
_____
_____

3. Tell me how to care for a pet of your choice.

_____
_____
_____

 **PERSONAL PRACTICE**

Use one of the writing prompts on this page, or think of your own topic. Then write an introductory paragraph that informs, describes, or persuades. What question could you use to begin each of these paragraphs?

# WRITING THE BODY: DEVELOPING TOPIC SENTENCES

Each of the three paragraphs in the body of your writing will include a topic sentence. The three topic sentences will clarify and expand on the subtopics presented in the introduction. The following excerpts that might be found in a political pamphlet demonstrate how this is done. The subtopics presented in the introduction are underlined for clarity.

Introduction
Proposition 1932A states that all junk mail be banned from delivery in the United States. If this proposition is voted into law, we would no longer need to thumb through stacks of fliers and envelopes we don't want just to read the mail we actually desire. Vote for Proposition 1932A and say no to growing garbage, depleted forests, and privacy intrusion.

Body Paragraph 1 Topic Sentence
The countless pieces of junk mail that get trashed every day in homes around the nation add to the increasing overflow at landfills all over America.

Body Paragraph 2 Topic Sentence
While junk mail adds to landfills, it depletes our nation's old growth forests by requiring the production of more and more paper products.

Body Paragraph 3 Topic Sentence
While the creation of junk mail takes trees away from our environment, the distribution of it takes privacy away from our citizens.

A topic sentence can be the first or the last sentence in a body paragraph. Most often, it is the first.

Sample
The most powerful scene in *Babe* is the one in which Farmer Hoggit dances for his pig. Displaying a reserved personality up to that point, the farmer comes to life when his wife is away and his sick pig needs some cheering. In a quiet but unsubtle manner, the viewer is made aware that Farmer Hoggit is experiencing growth. This awareness helps the viewer identify with Hoggit and at the same time serves as foreshadowing of more unorthodox behaviors to come.

Name _____ Date _____

WRITING THE BODY: DEVELOPING TOPIC SENTENCES

Directions: Develop the subtopics presented in the following thesis statements into three topic sentences that could introduce the three body paragraphs of a paper supporting the thesis. Look to the sample on the previous page if you need help getting started.

Thesis Statement: Living in the country is better than living in the city. Country living is more beautiful, less crowded, and more enjoyable than city living.

Body 1 Topic Sentence

_____

_____

Body 2 Topic Sentence

_____

_____

Body 3 Topic Sentence

_____

_____

Thesis Statement: Living in the city is better than living in the country. The city offers residents convenience, culture, and action.

Body 1 Topic Sentence

_____

_____

Body 2 Topic Sentence

_____

_____

Body 3 Topic Sentence

_____

_____

Published by Frank Schaffer Publication. Copyright protected.   31   0-7696-3402-8 *Writing with the Five-Paragraph Model*

WRITING THE BODY: USING DETAILS

Supporting statements prove the topic sentences in your three body paragraphs. Deciding what to use for support can be challenging, especially if your research yielded lots and lots of facts. One way to support a topic sentence is by listing specific details in your supporting sentences. This is especially effective when used in descriptive writing.

In the sample below, notice how the underlined subtopic sentence makes a statement and the body paragraph expands on the statement with descriptive details.

Prompt: Describe your house.

Introductory Paragraph
My house is a hodgepodge of beauty and horror. My recently remodeled living room is kept spotless. My kitchen is a picture of organized chaos. And my bedroom is a pig sty.

Sample Third Paragraph Body: Topic Sentence Supported by Details
My bedroom is a mess. Wrinkled shirts and dirty socks smell as lovely as they look draped over lamps and stereos, desktops and open cabinets. Paper scraps stick to glue drippings beside countless images cut from my stackless mounds of magazines. Unidentifiable crumbs, liquids, and food chunks cover my unmade bed. My mom calls my room the Harbor of Horror!

Name _____ Date _____

WRITING THE BODY: USING DETAILS

Directions: Develop the topic sentences below into full paragraphs by expanding the statement with descriptive details.

1. The food in our school cafeteria is uneatable.

_____
_____
_____

2. The house was haunted.

_____
_____
_____

3. My attic is a cluttered mess.

_____
_____
_____

PERSONAL PRACTICE

Think of a topic sentence. Then write it and enough descriptive details to make a full paragraph. Ask a friend to do the same. After you've both finished writing, read each other's paragraph.

Published by Frank Schaffer Publication. Copyright protected.　　33　　0-7696-3402-8 *Writing with the Five-Paragraph Model*

Writing the Body: Using Examples

Writing detailed supporting sentences is one way to prove the topic sentences in the body of your paper. Another way to support your body's topic sentences is to provide examples. This approach can be especially effective in persuasive and explanatory works.

Sample Explanatory Body Paragraph Supported with Examples

Teachers can implement one of several methods in the teaching of reading. For example, some teachers emphasize the sounds of letters and letter groups in a method called phonics. Some instructors build on the teaching of several basic sight words. Still others employ an approach wherein students follow along as a proficient reader reads a story over and over again.

Sample Persuasive Body Paragraph Supported with Examples

Exercising regularly has many benefits. For example, aerobic workouts can contribute to a healthy heart. Anaerobic movements build muscles. Playing team sports builds camaraderie. Even simple daily walks are believed to reduce stress and help you maintain a healthy weight. The many benefits of exercise far outweigh its drawbacks.

Name _____   Date _____

 **WRITING THE BODY: USING EXAMPLES**

Directions: Write a topic sentence to match the examples provided in this paragraph.

For example, he wrote essays and books. He experimented with electricity and ocean currents. He founded Philadelphia's first hospital and library. He served as postmaster to the colonies, diplomat to France, and delegate at the Constitutional Convention. Benjamin Franklin had his fingers in so many pies he was one of the most influential citizens this nation has ever known.

_____
_____
_____
_____

 **PERSONAL PRACTICE**

Develop the following topic sentences into complete paragraphs using examples as support.

Countless animals can make great indoor pets.

You can watch hundreds of cartoon programs on television these days.

# Writing the Body: Using Sequencing

Yet another way to organize supporting sentences in the body of your paper is through **sequencing.** When you sequence, you build a case for your topic sentence by listing facts in a sensible order. This order may be chronological or spatial. Sequencing works well when giving directions, chronicling a life or event, or describing a scene. Transitional words in chronologically sequenced paragraphs include *first, second, next, then,* and *finally*. Transitional words in spatially sequenced paragraphs include *here, there, behind, in front of,* and *beside*.

Sequencing Directions
Baking bread is a long process. First you mix the ingredients. Then you knead the dough. Next you let the dough rise. Once it has risen, you punch it down and let it rise again. Finally you bake the bread.

Sequencing an Event
The new boy took two broad coppers out of his pocket and held them out with derision. Tom struck them to the ground. In an instant both boys were rolling and tumbling in the dirt, gripped together like cats; and for the space of a minute they tugged and tore at each other's hair and clothes, punched and scratched each other's nose, and covered themselves with dust and glory. Presently the confusion took form, and through the fog of battle Tom appeared, seated astride the new boy, and pounding him with his fists. "Holler 'nuff!" said he.

—Mark Twain, *The Adventures of Tom Sawyer*

Sequencing a Life
Jimmy Stewart lived an interesting life. He was born to a hardware salesman in Pennsylvania. After earning good grades in elementary and high school, he went on to earn honors from Princeton. He thought of becoming an architect but did some summer acting instead. His summer acting turned into a lifetime career. In 1985, he was awarded a special Oscar for "50 years of meaningful performances."

Sequencing a Scene
Our English classroom is like a complete library. On the walls hang quotes from famous authors. On the side shelves you can find literary books. In the back of the room are reference books and other nonfiction works. Beside the teacher's desk is a computer with an Internet connection and bookmarks marking web pages of hundreds of famous authors. Everywhere you look you are reminded of the importance of reading.

Name _____ Date _____

WRITING THE BODY: USING SEQUENCING

Directions: Write a topic sentence for the sequential paragraph here.

Before you can even begin your paper, you need to evaluate the assignment. Then you have to research your topic. After you brainstorm and organize your information, you are ready to write. Start with your introductory paragraph. Introduce your thesis in an exciting way. Then move on to the body of your paper. Write topic sentences based on the subtopics mentioned in your introduction. Be sure your topic sentences are well supported. Finally, conclude your paper with a judgment or summary.

_____
_____
_____

PERSONAL PRACTICE

Write a chronological paragraph about your life.

Write a sequencing paragraph about everything you did yesterday.

Write a sequencing paragraph explaining how to do something (e.g., apply makeup, perform an Ollie on a skateboard, make cookies).

Writing the Body: Using Importance and Necessity

An effective means of organizing supporting sentences in a persuasive paragraph is in **order of importance.** Doing so helps build support for little points before making the big point. It also helps build suspense.

Sample

Charlotte's Web is a marvelous children's story. E. B. White's writing style is elegant and engaging. The story's characters are lifelike and enduring. Most importantly, *Charlotte's Web* gently addresses the important childhood themes of loss, love, life, and death.

Writing in **order of necessity** is like laying the bricks for a house. Paragraphs written in the order of necessity build one argument upon another. Sentences that appear later in the paragraph rely on the presence of sentences before them to make sense.

This paragraph from the Declaration of Independence is structured in order of necessity. Notice that arguments of the second and third sentences rely on, refer to, and build on the statement made in the first sentence. The statements of the fifth sentence build on those made in the fourth sentence. (Sentences have been numbered for convenience.)

1 We hold these truths to be self-evident, that all men are created equal, that they are endowed by their Creator with certain unalienable Rights, that among these are Life, Liberty, and the pursuit of Happiness. **2** That to secure these rights, Governments are instituted among Men, deriving their just powers from the consent of the governed. **3** That whenever any Form of Government becomes destructive of these ends, it is the Right of the People to alter or abolish it, and to institute new Government, laying its foundation on such principles and organizing its powers in such form, as to them shall seem most likely to effect their Safety and Happiness. **4** Prudence, indeed, will dictate that Governments long established should not be changed for light and transient causes; and accordingly all experience hath shewn, that mankind are more disposed to suffer, while evils are sufferable, than to right themselves by abolishing the forms to which they are accustomed. **5** But when a long train of abuses and usurpations, pursuing invariably the same Object evinces a design to reduce them under absolute Despotism, it is their right, it is their duty, to throw off such Government, and to provide new Guards for their future security . . .

Name _____ Date _____

 **Writing the Body: Using Importance and Necessity**

Directions: Analyze the classic paragraphs below by answering the questions that follow each.

I intend that this autobiography shall become a model for all future autobiographies when it is published, after my death, and I also intend that it shall be read and admired a good many centuries because of its form and method—a form and method whereby the past and the present are constantly brought face to face, resulting in contrasts which newly fire up the interest all along, like contact of flint with steel. Moreover, this autobiography of mine does not select from my life its showy episodes, but deals mainly in the common experiences which make up the life of the average human being, because these episodes are of a sort which he is familiar with in his own life, and in which he sees his own life reflected and set down in print. The usual, conventional autobiographer seems to particularly hunt out those occasions in his career when he came into contact with celebrated persons, whereas his contacts with the uncelebrated were just as interesting to him, and would be to his reader, and were vastly more numerous than his collisions with the famous.

—Mark Twain, *Chapters from My Autobiography*

1. This paragraph is written in order of importance. In what two major ways does Mark Twain argue that his autobiography differs from traditional autobiographies? What clue word in the middle of the paragraph hints that the second way is of more consequence to Twain?

The Law of the Jungle, which never orders anything without reason, forbids every beast to eat Man except when he is killing to show his children how to kill, and then he must hunt outside the hunting grounds of his pack or tribe. The real reason for this is that man-killing means, sooner or later, the arrival of white men on elephants, with guns, and hundreds of brown men with gongs and rockets and torches. Then everybody in the jungle suffers. The reason the beasts give among themselves is that Man is the weakest and most defenseless of all living things, and it is unsportsmanlike to touch him. They say too—and it is true—that man-eaters become mangy and lose their teeth.

—Rudyard Kipling, *Jungle Book*, "Mowgli's Brothers"

2. This paragraph is written in order of necessity. Explain how each consecutive sentence builds on the one before it right up to the end of the paragraph.

Writing the Conclusion

Summarizing
The most basic concluding paragraph style simply summarizes the paper. Conclusions that summarize look much like introductions.

Sample
Professional basketball, then, makes for an exciting spectator sport. The rules of the game create a fast-paced setting. The graceful feats of the game's tree-top players dazzle and amaze. The game's huge fan base adds color, energy, and excitement to the already enticing sport.

Making Judgments
A more sophisticated conclusion style offers judgments about the facts presented. Concluding judgments should be clearly based on statements made in the body of the paper. Leading statements throughout the work often foreshadow concluding judgments.

Sample
Leonardo de Vinci was perhaps the most influential figure of the Italian Renaissance. His contributions to art, science, and architecture were invaluable in and of themselves. Taken as a whole, they were accomplishments in such diverse fields that they defined the Renaissance period.

Pointing Beyond the Paper
Another sophisticated conclusion style points the reader beyond the paper. A conclusion must never introduce a new topic, but it may effectively expand on a thesis or suggest an action based on facts and argument presented earlier in the work.

Sample
Groundhog Day is a priceless movie. Its intentionally repetitive plot is miraculously fresh and well-structured. Its characters experience significant but believable growth. Its theme is sound and important. Buy a copy of *Groundhog Day* today and share it with your family over and over again.

Name _____ Date _____

WRITING THE CONCLUSION

Directions: Which of the following statements found in conclusions *summarize*, *make a judgment*, and *point beyond the paper*? Indicate your responses on the lines provided.

_____ 1. Jupiter is definitely the most fascinating planet.

_____ 2. Taking care of a pet is time-consuming, difficult, and worth it.

_____ 3. My summer vacation activities included fun in the water, fun in the woods, and fun in the sun.

_____ 4. So don't buy a used car.

_____ 5. Those are the things that make a best friend the best.

_____ 6. Write your congressman and make a difference.

_____ 7. There is no better sport to watch or play.

_____ 8. Don't watch the movie. Don't read the book. Don't even bother.

_____ 9. Shane weighs in as a complex character whose attributes far outweigh his faults.

_____ 10. What goes on in the world of ants is really a microcosm of what goes on in the ecological web at large.

Directions: Write a concluding paragraph that fits one of the styles described. Switch papers with a classmate. Can you guess each other's style?

_____
_____
_____
_____
_____

Published by Frank Schaffer Publication. Copyright protected.   41   0-7696-3402-8 *Writing with the Five-Paragraph Model*

Writing the Conclusion: Combining Styles

Often writings combine statements of summary, judgment, and expansion in the conclusion. This approach is effective since it orients readers to previous points in statements of summary before trying to convince them of specific judgments or asking them to take action.

In this excerpt from Abraham Lincoln's speech at the fourth debate of the Lincoln-Douglas debates, the statements of summary have been underlined, the statements of judgment are in italics, and the statements that point beyond the speech are written in bold.

Sample

Now, I want to come back to my original question. Trumbull says that Judge Douglas had a bill with a provision in it for submitting a Constitution to be put to a vote of the people of Kansas. **Does Judge Douglas deny that fact? Does he deny that the provision which Trumbull reads was put in the bill?** Then Trumbull says he struck it out. **Does he have to deny that?** He does not, and I have the right to repeat the question—why Judge Douglas took it out . . . *When he will not tell what the true reason was, he stands in the attitude of an accused thief who has stolen goods in his possession, and when called to account, refuses to tell where he got them.* . . . **Now I ask what is the reason Judge Douglas is so chary about coming to the exact question?** *If he explains his actions on this question . . . it will be satisfactory. But until he does that—until he gives a better or more plausible reason than he has offered against the evidence in the case, I suggest to him it will not avail him at all that he swells himself up, takes on dignity, and calls people liars.*

Name _____ Date _____

Writing the Conclusion: Combining Styles

Stephen Douglas structured the conclusion of his speech in the seventh of the Lincoln-Douglas debates to utter a statement of summary followed by a statement pointing beyond the speech to a statement of judgment and so on.

Directions: Decide which of the statements in this concluding paragraph are statements of summary, statements of judgment, and statements leading the listener beyond the speech. Then record them on the lines provided below.

My friends, if, as I have said before, we will only live up to this great fundamental principle, there will be peace between the North and the South. Mr. Lincoln admits that under the Constitution on all domestic questions, except slavery, we ought not to interfere with the people of each State. What right have we to interfere with slavery any more than we have to interfere with any other question? He says that this slavery question is now the bone of contention. Why? Simply because agitators have combined in all the free States to make war upon it. Suppose the agitators in the States should combine in one-half of the Union to make war upon the railroad system of the other half. They would thus be driven to the same sectional strife. Suppose one section makes war upon any other peculiar institution of the opposite section, and the same strife is produced. The only remedy and safety is that we shall stand by the Constitution as our fathers made it, obey the laws as they are passed, while they stand the proper test and sustain the decisions of the Supreme Court and the constituted authorities.

Summary Statements

_____

_____

_____

Judgment Statements

_____

_____

_____

Leading Statements

_____

_____

_____

Analyzing the Five-Paragraph Model

Directions: Now that you have mastered the elements of a five-paragraph writing, take a look at them together. Read the following with an eye on the various elements of a five-paragraph writing.

On March 4, 1877, Elizabeth Morgan—a former slave—and her husband, Sydney, welcomed the seventh of their eleven children into the world. Little was probably expected from Garrett Augustus Morgan. After all, he had none of the privileges of wealth, and his family's poverty required Garrett to spend more time in the fields than in the classroom as a child. Just the same, Garrett did make something of his life thanks to his determination, innovation, and heroism.

Determined to succeed from an early age, Garrett left home at 14 in search of employment. At first he worked as a handyman and then as a sewing machine repairman. By 1907, his solid work ethic had catapulted him to the position of owner of his own sewing machine equipment and repair shop. Soon he owned a tailoring shop and distributed hair care products as well.

In each of his jobs, Garrett demonstrated amazing innovation. While working as a repairman, he invented a sewing machine belt fastener. While he owned the sewing machine repair shop, he invented a zigzag sewing attachment. As a tailor, he and his 32 employees sewed clothing on equipment Garrett invented and built. And the hair care products Garrett distributed were—you guessed it—of his own invention.

By 1914, Garrett had shifted his innovative genius to more heroic inventions. After witnessing an accident between a horse-drawn carriage and a car, he invented a traffic light. After watching firemen die of smoke inhalation, he invented a safety helmet, even donning the new device himself to rescue workmen trapped in an underground tunnel explosion. When World War I soldiers needed a gas mask, Garrett refined the safety mask for that use.

Garrett's lifetime accomplishments did not go unnoticed. His traffic light invention earned him a government citation and $40,000. His heroic rescue of trapped tunnel workmen earned him national fame. His safety mask and gas mask both earned gold medals from international organizations. Garrett Augustus Morgan's determination, innovation, and heroism carried him from a place of poverty and little schooling to one of fame, wealth, and respect.

Name _____ Date _____

ANALYZING THE FIVE-PARAGRAPH MODEL

Directions: Answer the following multiple-choice questions designed to help you analyze the informative report on Garrett Augustus Morgan. Indicate your responses by circling the letter representing the best choice.

1. The introductory paragraph begins with . . .

    a. a quote.

    b. an anecdote.

    c. a thesis statement.

    d. a question.

2. The three subtopics addressed in the body of the paper include . . .

    a. Garrett's inventions, business skills, and heroism.

    b. Garrett's home life, work life, and inventions.

    c. Garrett's determination, innovation, and heroism.

    d. Garrett's childhood, adulthood, and old age.

3. The first paragraph of the paper's body is organized . . .

    a. chronologically.

    b. in order of importance.

    c. in order of necessity.

    d. using comparisons.

4. The topic sentence of the second paragraph of the paper's body . . .

    a. appears at the end of the paragraph.

    b. is supported by examples.

    c. appears in the middle of the sentence.

    d. is supported by facts listed in order of importance.

5. The topic sentence of the concluding paragraph . . .

    a. appears at the end of the paragraph.

    b. summarizes the paper, restating the theme.

    c. is supported by details.

    d. all of the above.

DESCRIPTIVE WRITING: RECORD AND WRITE

Describing a place is a great way to practice the five-paragraph writing model. Places have sights, sounds, smells, and textures. Places can be associated with people, events, and memories.

Directions: Think of a place that has special meaning to you. It can be a vacation spot you have visited once or a favorite room in your house that you frequent every day. Choose a place that has lots of associations for you. Use the brainstorming map below to prepare you to complete the five-paragraph paper on the following page.

Name the place _____

Physical Associations

Sounds of the Place
_____
_____
_____

Sights of the Place
_____
_____
_____

Smells of the Place
_____
_____
_____

Textures of the Place
_____
_____
_____

Emotional Associations

Feelings I Have About the Place
_____
_____
_____

Experiences I've Had in the Place
_____
_____
_____

People I Associate with the Place
_____
_____
_____

Name _____ Date _____

Descriptive Writing: Record and Write

Directions: You have compiled lists of impressions about your favorite place. There are several possible ways to organize your ideas, but for the sake of this practice paper, you will divide impressions into physical and emotional ones. The physical descriptions of your place will give general introductory and concluding information. The emotional descriptions will make up the body of your work. Fill in the blanks below to write your paper. You can add other details as needed.

1. One of my favorite places on earth is _____. It is (general description) _____
_____.

2. It is special to me because I associate it with people, experiences, and feelings that are important to me. The person/people I associate with (name of place) _____
is/are _____
_____.

3. This person is/These people are important to me because _____
_____.

4. I associate my favorite places with many special experiences. One time _____
_____.

5. Another time _____.

6. Perhaps most important are the feelings I associate with my favorite place. My place makes me feel _____ because _____
_____.

7. It also makes me feel _____ because _____
_____.

8. Sometimes it even makes me feel _____ because _____
_____.

9. I love (name of place) _____. It makes me think of special people, experiences, and feelings. _____ (Name of place) will always mean something to me.

Evaluating Fiction: Analyzing Aesop

Directions: Study the following fables written by Aesop and translated by George Fyler Townsend in the 1800s. They will be the basis of a five-paragraph writing you will complete with assistance.

The Donkey and the Grasshoppers
A Donkey having heard some Grasshoppers chirping, was highly enchanted; and desiring to possess the same charms of melody, demanded what sort of food they lived on to give them such beautiful voices. They replied, "The dew." The Donkey resolved that he would live only upon dew, and in a short time died of hunger.

The Kites and the Swans
The Kites of olden times, as well as the Swans, had the privilege of song. But having heard the neigh of the horse, they were so enchanted with the sound, they tried to imitate it; and in trying to neigh, they forgot how to sing.

The Crab and the Fox
A Crab, forsaking the seashore, chose a neighboring green meadow as its feeding ground. A Fox came across him, and being very hungry ate him up. Just as he was on the point of being eaten, the Crab said, "I well deserve my fate, for what business had I on the land, when by my nature and habits I am only adapted for the sea?"

The Crow and the Raven
A Crow was jealous of the Raven, because he was considered a bird of good omen and always attracted the attention of men, who noted by his flight the good or evil course of future events. Seeing some travelers approaching, the Crow flew up into the tree, and perching herself on one of the branches, cawed as loudly as she could. The travelers turned towards the sound and wondered what it foreboded, when one of them said to his companion, "Let us proceed on our journey, my friend, for it is only the caw of a crow, and her cry, you know, is no omen."

Name _____ Date _____

Evaluating Fiction: ANALYZING AESOP

Directions: Write a five-paragraph paper discussing the common moral of the four presented fables using the introduction provided as well as the stated starter sentences for each of the other paragraphs.

Aesop's Warning

A donkey dies of hunger. Kites and swans lose their singing voices. A crab gets eaten alive. A crow gets mocked and ignored. The four fables presented here all issue a warning. What they warn against is envy, shame, and the decision to act against one's nature.

1. In each of the four fables, envy is the beginning of the trouble for an animal who encounters a terrible fate.

_____

_____

2. The envy each ill-fated animal feels grows out of a lack of pride in himself.

_____

_____

3. Although envy and shame start the trouble, a decision against being oneself is what seals the fate of the animals in Aesop's four fables.

_____

_____

Aesop's four fables offer a warning not only to his animal characters but to all of us.

Evaluating Nonfiction: Behind Every Great Man

After Hanna Penn's husband, William, suffered a disabling stroke, Hanna negotiated deals that saved Pennsylvania from bankruptcy. Later she settled an important land dispute between her founding husband's colony and Maryland. Have you ever heard of Hanna Penn? Probably not. "Behind every great man," an adage contends, "is a great woman," but history books don't seem to care. Consider the hidden contributions of Constanze Mozart, Mary Leakey, and Emily Roebling.

Wolfgang Amadeus Mozart, of course, was a musical genius. At the age of four he toured Europe playing the violin and organ. He wrote technically perfect and creatively inspiring compositions throughout his life. Alas, Mozart was a lousy businessman and a somewhat confrontational personality. By the time of his death, his genius had brought him neither success nor wealth. Thanks to Mozart's wife, Constanze, however, he did achieve his well-deserved fame posthumously. She sold his works, arranged the writing of his biography, and arranged the playing of his pieces after her husband had died. Thanks to those choices, we know of the genius of Mozart today.

Louis Leakey was a famous anthropologist. His discovery of a skull in 1959 provided the missing link to a period of prehistory 1.75 million years old. Louis was greatly celebrated for his discovery. Only it wasn't his. His wife, Mary, discovered the famous skull and went on to achieve other greats in the field of anthropology following the death of her husband—and the truth of her discovery—in 1972.

Emily Roebling's husband never achieved the level of fame of Mr. Mozart or even Mr. Leakey, but he was well respected in New York City. As the chief engineer of the Brooklyn Bridge project, Washington Roebling was working on the then-longest suspension bridge in the world when he fell ill. Emily oversaw the completion of the bridge when her husband was confined to bed. Washington appreciated his wife's contribution and insisted she be the first person to cross the bridge, but did you read about the event in your history book? Probably not.

Traditionally, history has been quiet about the accomplishments of women. Due to a lack of legal rights in the past, their contributions have often been behind-the-scenes achievements. In today's more enlightened culture, it is high time we give them center stage.

Name _____ Date _____

Evaluating Nonfiction: Behind Every Great Man

Directions: Write a five-paragraph paper discussing the theme, purpose, and intended audience of "Behind Every Great Man." Use the introduction provided as well as the stated starter sentences for each of the other paragraphs.

You've just read about behind-the-scenes accomplishments of women in history. What were you expected to get out of what you read? Were you supposed to be entertained? Informed? Convinced? An evaluation of the intended audience, theme, and purpose of a work can help you get the most out of what you read.

Women: Center Stage
Several categories of people likely are the intended audience of "Behind Every Great Man." (*Note:* Consider politicians, historians, educators, students, and textbook editors.)

_____

_____

_____

The theme of "Behind Every Great Man" suggests that women's accomplishments have been ignored by historians.

_____

_____

_____

The purpose of "Behind Every Great Man" is one of persuasion.

_____

_____

_____

Knowing the audience, theme, and purpose associated with a work can assist a reader in getting the most out of a document.

_____

_____

_____

WRITING A REPORT

Directions: Study the following facts about Jamaica. Consider which three facts are general enough to use for an introduction to a paper called *Jamaica*. What three categories might the other facts comprise?

Jamaica is an island located in the Caribbean Sea.

Sugar, tropical fruit, coffee, cacao, and spices are exported from Jamaica.

Jamaica was discovered by Columbus and claimed as Spanish territory in 1494.

Jamaica is one of a chain of islands called the West Indies.

The British captured Jamaica from the Spanish in 1655.

Aluminum is mined and oil refined in Jamaica.

Jamaica is home to approximately 2,500,000 people.

Jamaica and other West Indies islands formed the West Indies Federation in 1858.

Jamaica makes a good deal of its money from tourism.

Most people who live in Jamaica today are of African descent.

Jamaican industries include textiles, printing, and chemicals.

Most Jamaicans are Christians.

Today, Jamaica is an independent nation governed by a prime minister and elected legislative representatives.

Jamaica gained its independence in 1962.

Jamaicans speak English and Creole.

When the island's natives died out, African slaves were moved to Jamaica to work the sugarcane fields.

Name _____ Date _____

WRITING A REPORT

Directions: Complete the following five-paragraph writing about Jamaica. The last lines of the introduction and conclusion have been provided as well as the first lines of each body paragraph. Use the facts on the previous page to help you write your report. Organize and rephrase them in ways that work for you.

Jamaica

_____

_____

A general introduction to Jamaica includes information on its history, its people, and its economy.

In 1494, Columbus discovered Jamaica and claimed it to be Spanish territory.

_____

_____

_____

Jamaica today is populated primarily by African descendents.

_____

_____

_____

Jamaica's economy depends on industry, agriculture, and tourism.

_____

_____

_____

_____

_____

Visit Jamaica and learn even more.

Descriptive Writing

You have been guided through a practice descriptive writing. Now it is time to try your hand at a five-paragraph descriptive writing.

Directions: Choose one of the prompts on this page. Complete the prewriting activity on the next page. Then write a five-paragraph work on your own paper.

Descriptive Writing Options

Tell about your best friend.

Describe your house.

Write about going to the fair.

Write a paper about the experiences of a typical school day.

Tell about your favorite relative.

Summarize a book or movie.

Tell about different styles of music, art, or dance.

Describe a sport.

Describe your dream park.

Tell about an experience you have had at an amusement park.

Describe a place without ever naming it.

Describe an animal without ever naming it.

Explain how to accomplish a task of your choice.

Name _____ Date _____

DESCRIPTIVE WRITING

Write a thesis statement: _____

_____

How will you introduce your thesis?
Circle one: anecdote   quotation   question   other

Write 12 phrases that prove your thesis statement.

1. _____   7. _____
2. _____   8. _____
3. _____   9. _____
4. _____   10. _____
5. _____   11. _____
6. _____   12. _____

Divide your 12 proves into three subtopics.

Subtopic 1: _____

1. _____   3. _____
2. _____   4. _____

Subtopic 2: _____

1. _____   3. _____
2. _____   4. _____

Subtopic 3: _____

1. _____   3. _____
2. _____   4. _____

How will you organize your paragraphs? Circle one or more:
   details   examples   order of importance   order of necessity

How will your paper conclude? Circle one or more:
   summarize   judge   lead beyond

List any references you used here:

_____

_____

Evaluating Fiction

You have been guided through evaluating fiction. Now it is time to try your hand at a five-paragraph fiction evaluation.

Directions: Choose one of the prompts on this page. Complete the prewriting activity on the next page. Then write a five-paragraph work on your own paper.

Fiction Evaluation Options

Compare a movie you have seen with a book version of the same story that you have read.

Analyze your favorite character from a movie or a book.

Write about the symbolism in a poem of your choice.

Talk about the figurative language in a short story of your choice.

Explain the importance of setting in a novel you have read.

Think of a book you did not like reading. Tell why you did not like the book.

Write a review of the last television program you watched.

Explain the elements of drama.

Compare and contrast two books by the same author.

Compare and contrast the writings of two different authors.

Compare the elements of poetry, drama, and fiction.

Define writing style. Use examples of several authors' unique styles.

Write a book report.

Talk about the moral or theme of a short story.

Tell why you like or do not like reading short stories or novels.

Name _____   Date _____

Evaluating Fiction

Write a thesis statement: _____
_____

How will you introduce your thesis?
Circle one: anecdote   quotation   question   other

Write 12 phrases that prove your thesis statement.

1. _____   7. _____
2. _____   8. _____
3. _____   9. _____
4. _____   10. _____
5. _____   11. _____
6. _____   12. _____

Divide your 12 proves into three subtopics.

Subtopic 1: _____

1. _____   3. _____
2. _____   4. _____

Subtopic 2: _____

1. _____   3. _____
2. _____   4. _____

Subtopic 3: _____

1. _____   3. _____
2. _____   4. _____

How will you organize your paragraphs? Circle one or more:
   details   examples   order of importance   order of necessity

How will your paper conclude? Circle one or more:
   summarize   judge   lead beyond

List any references you used here:

_____
_____

Published by Frank Schaffer Publication. Copyright protected.   0-7696-3402-8 *Writing with the Five-Paragraph Model*

Evaluating Nonfiction

You have been guided through a practice evaluation of nonfiction. Now it is time to try your hand at a five-paragraph nonfiction evaluation.

Directions: Choose one of the prompts on this page. Complete the prewriting activity on the next page. Then write a five-paragraph work on your own paper.

Nonfiction Evaluation Options

Summarize a newspaper article.

Compare and contrast fact and opinion.

Tell why you agree or disagree with a newspaper, radio, or televised editorial.

Write a review of a documentary.

Tell what you learned from the last nonfiction movie you watched in class.

Write a report on a nonfiction book.

Write a report on a nonfiction magazine article.

Tell why you like or dislike biographies.

Read a biography of a famous personality. Write about what you learned.

Compare and contrast television, radio, and newspaper coverage of a current event.

Give your opinions about a controversial issue in the news today.

Write a review of your school newspaper or another newspaper.

Determine the purpose, theme, and intended audience of a magazine article.

Compare a documentary with a biography.

Name _____ Date _____

Evaluating Nonfiction

Write a thesis statement: _____
_____

How will you introduce your thesis?
Circle one: anecdote   quotation   question   other

Write 12 phrases that prove your thesis statement.

1. _____   7. _____
2. _____   8. _____
3. _____   9. _____
4. _____   10. _____
5. _____   11. _____
6. _____   12. _____

Divide your 12 proves into three subtopics.

Subtopic 1: _____

1. _____   3. _____
2. _____   4. _____

Subtopic 2: _____

1. _____   3. _____
2. _____   4. _____

Subtopic 3: _____

1. _____   3. _____
2. _____   4. _____

How will you organize your paragraphs? Circle one or more:
   details   examples   order of importance   order of necessity

How will your paper conclude? Circle one or more:
   summarize   judge   lead beyond

List any references you used here:
_____
_____

WRITING A REPORT

You have been guided through the writing of a practice report. Now it is time to try your hand at a five-paragraph report.

Directions: Choose one of the prompts on this page. Complete the prewriting activity on the next page. Then write a five-paragraph work on your own paper.

Report Options

Report on your home city or state.

Report on the history of your school.

Report on your favorite actor or singer.

Report on a personality from American history.

Report on a famous political event from history.

Report on an invention.

Report on minority contributions to society.

Report on women's contributions to society.

Report on an author.

Report on a business or institution.

Report on a sport or an athlete.

Report on learning styles or types of intelligence.

Write a report that includes statistics.

Write a report that includes comments of someone you interview.

Write about a time period in history.

Name _____ Date _____

WRITING A REPORT

Directions: Research your topic and create notecards according to the suggestions on pages 16–17.

Write a thesis statement: _____
_____

How will you introduce your thesis?
Circle one: anecdote   quotation   question   other

Write 12 phrases that prove your thesis statement.

1. _____   7. _____
2. _____   8. _____
3. _____   9. _____
4. _____   10. _____
5. _____   11. _____
6. _____   12. _____

Divide your 12 proves into three subtopics.

Subtopic 1: _____

1. _____   3. _____
2. _____   4. _____

Subtopic 2: _____

1. _____   3. _____
2. _____   4. _____

Subtopic 3: _____

1. _____   3. _____
2. _____   4. _____

How will your paper conclude? Circle one or more:
   summarize   judge   lead beyond

List any references you used here:
_____
_____

How Did I Do?

You now have a lot of practice with five-paragraph works. Below are a number of sentence starters and completing phrases. Circle all of the completing phrases that apply to you. This will help your teacher discover what you have mastered and what you are still learning.

I know . . .
what a paragraph is.
what a five-paragraph writing is.
what a thesis is.
three or more ways to start an introduction.
what a subtopic is.
how to research information.
how to organize ideas into topics and subtopics.
the purpose of body paragraphs.
three or more ways to organize a body paragraph.
three styles of conclusion.

I am good at . . .
researching a topic.
organizing ideas into topics and subtopics.
writing effective introductions.
writing thesis statements.
writing topic sentences.
writing body paragraphs.
writing effective conclusions.

I need help . . .
with research.
organizing my ideas.
writing effective introductions.
writing thesis statements.
writing topic sentences.
writing body paragraphs.
writing effective conclusions.

I like or don't like writing five-paragraph works because . . .

Go Team!

Below are a number of sentence starters and completing phrases about teamwork. Circle all of the completing phrases that apply to you and your group.

I was good at . . .
following the teacher's directions.
listening to my team members.
taking direction from my team members.
communicating my ideas with my team members.
doing my fair share of the work.
helping my team keep focused.
helping my team reach agreement when we disagreed.
including everyone in my team in our project.

I could have been better at . . .
following the teacher's directions.
listening to my team members.
taking direction from my team members.
communicating my ideas with my team members.
doing my fair share of the work.
helping my team keep focused.
helping my team reach agreement when we disagreed.
including everyone in my team in our project.

Rate the following on a scale of one to ten.

My participation in our group:
1   2   3   4   5   6   7   8   9   10

My group's ability to stay focused:
1   2   3   4   5   6   7   8   9   10

My group's ability to get along:
1   2   3   4   5   6   7   8   9   10

My group's ability to divide work evenly:
1   2   3   4   5   6   7   8   9   10

The end result of my group's project:
1   2   3   4   5   6   7   8   9   10

Answer Key

Many activities in *Writing with the Five-Paragraph Model* are open-ended. This answer key is provided for those questions that require specific responses.

What Is a Paragraph?..................................page 7
1. "Saturday morning was come, and all the summer world was bright and fresh, and brimming with life."
2. the joys of summer
3. provide details
4. Cardiff Hill

What Is the Five-Paragraph Model?..................page 9
1. An introductory paragraph introduces a topic and three subtopics.
2. The body consists of three paragraphs that support the subtopics of the introduction.
3. The conclusion ties the work together.
4. Langston Hughes wanted to write about the black experience. So he did.
5. wrote essays about black issues; wrote plays, novels, and short stories about the black experience; wrote jazz-style poetry
6. wrote jazz-style poetry
7. gracious, honest, and beautiful examination of black American experience

The Five-Paragraph Writing Process...................page 11
1. evaluate the assignment, research your topic, brainstorm, organize
2. Possible answers include using an encyclopedia, biography, autobiography, web site, or televised documentary.
3. the book *Charlotte's Web*
4. Answers will vary.
5. to help you know how to divide information into sensible paragraphs

Evaluating the Assignment..............................page 13
1. describe your bedroom, body
2. prove the existence of gravity, introduction
3. write a review of your favorite movie, conclusion
4. define the word *freedom*, body

Referencing Your Sources................................page 19
Gardner, Howard. *The Mind's New Science*. New York: Basic Books Inc., 1985.
Isbister, J. N. *Freud: An Introduction to His Life and Work*. New York: Polity Press, 1985.
Perry, Helen Swick. *Psychiatrist of America: The Life of Harry Stack Sullivan*. Cambridge, Massachusetts: Belknap Press, 1982.
Storr, Anthony, editor. *The Essential Jung*. Princeton, New Jersey: Princeton University Press, 1983.
Watson, John B. *Behaviorism*. New York: W. W. Norton and Company, 1958.

Writing the Body: Using Examples......................page 35
Benjamin Franklin's contributions to the birth of this nation were varied and important.

Writing the Body: Using Sequencing....................page 37
There are many steps involved in the preparation for and writing of a five-paragraph paper.

Writing the Body: Using Importance and Necessity..page 39
1. Twain argues his autobiography combines past and present and deals in common experiences. The word *moreover* lets you know which difference he finds more important.
2. The *Jungle Book* paragraph first states the law of the jungle. Then it gives the factual reason for it, the reason animals state for it, and as an afterthought, a secondary reason for it.

Writing the Conclusion...................................page 41
1. judgment
2. summarize
3. summarize
4. point beyond
5. summarize or judgment
6. point beyond
7. judgment
8. judgment or point beyond
9. judgment
10. summarize or judgment

Writing the Conclusion: Combining Styles...........page 43
Summary
My friends, if, as I have said before, we will only live up to this great fundamental principle, there will be peace between the North and the South.
Mr. Lincoln admits that under the Constitution on all domestic questions, except slavery, we ought not to interfere with the people of each State.
He says that this slavery question is now the bone of contention.
Judgment
Simply because agitators have combined in all the free States to make war upon it.
They would thus be driven to the same sectional strife.
The only remedy and safety is that we shall stand by the Constitution as our fathers made it, obey the laws as they are passed, while they stand the proper test and sustain the decisions of the Supreme Court and the constituted authorities.
Leading
What right have we to interfere with slavery any more than we have to interfere with any other question?
Why?
Suppose the agitators in the States should combine in one-half of the Union to make war upon the railroad system of the other half.
Suppose one section makes war upon any other peculiar institution of the opposite section, and the same strife is produced.

Analyzing the Five-Paragraph Model..................page 45
1. b
2. c
3. a
4. b
5. d